ON NEW STREET I SEE A MERMAID

ANNETTE ILES

First Published in Great Britain by Crystal Clear Books 2025

Copyright © Annette Iles, 2025

Annette Iles has asserted her moral right under the Copyright Design and Patents Act 1988 to be identified as the author of this work.

This book is a work of poetry and, except in the case of historical fact, any resemblance to actual persons, living or dead, is purely coincidental.

No paragraph of this publication may be reproduced, copied, stored or transmitted in any format save with written permission or in accordance with the provisions of the Copyright, Designs and Patents Act 1988, or under the terms of any license, permitting limited copying issued by the Copyright Licensing Agency, 33 Alfred Place, London, WC1E 7DP.

No part of this book may be used in any manner in the learning, training or development of generative artificial intelligence technologies (including but not limited to machine learning models and large language models whether by data scraping, data mining or use in any way to create or form a part of data sets or in any other way.

Published by: Crystal Clear Books: www.crystalclearbooks.co.uk

ISBN: 978-1-0684474-5-7

Cover Image: ID 18886956 | Sea © Geraktv | Dreamstime.com

FOR TERRY

Acknowledgements

Many of the poems in this pamphlet started life in the writing groups I belong to, in particular The Percival Guildhouse classes and NaPoWriMo17. So, grateful thanks must go to my wonderful writing companions, who provide inspiration, endless encouragement, and incisive feedback – and make writing poetry fun!

Thanks also to the team at Crystal Clear Books – Sue for her thoughtful and meticulous editing, and Linda for absolutely everything else, including the beautiful cover design.

Most of all, thank-you to Cathy Whittaker, poet and inspirational tutor, for opening my eyes to all the riches of poetry.

Contents

On Sea Lane Someone Is Playing The Piano 1
Waiting For Optimism 2
A Woman Who Does Not Believe In Spells 3
Talking About The Weather 4
Caff 5
Also On Connor Road 6
On New Street I See A Mermaid 7
Bird Feeders 8
Forgetting 9
Edge 10
The 15:30 To Birmingham 11
Another Conversation About Where I Should Live 12
Waves were for other kids 13
11 August 1999 14
Iona 15
Christmas Card From My Aunt 16
What Is Kept 17
Song For Midsummer 18
The Pottery Bowl Speaks 19
The Temperature In The Crater Lake 20
And What If He Does? 21
The Gentleman Of Fortune 22
Mrs Davies Is Well Enough To Leave The House 23
For Planting 24
You Know It Is Over 25
Rondeau For The Mirror 26
Things She Taught Me 27
For A Moment 28
Woman In The Distance 29
This Storm 30
The Day Of The Electrician 31
On the Matter of Perspectives 32
In February 33
We Make Soup 34
When you are sad 35

Field Notes..36
Open 37
Poetry Previously Published..38

On Sea Lane Someone Is Playing The Piano

Notes scatter through the drowsing afternoon
like handfuls of flung silver

they spill from where the houses
shrink to beach huts, that last cottage
the one with yellow windowsills and
a badly-parked builder's van

who, I wonder
a child practising? a salt-skinned woman
letting traces of sand fall on the keys
like tears? or maybe
it's the builder, sick of hammering
stopped for a mug of tea, some Chopin

the yellow door stands wide

I could peer in, I nearly do
yet what would I see?
only more small mysteries
unfathomable surfaces of other lives

I gather my imaginings
walk on towards the sea
little shoals of notes
swim with me.

Waiting For Optimism

I think it will look like May at 4 am
when, hours unslept, you realise
darkness has begun to shape
itself into angles and folds
it's too soon for certainties
you can't make out titles
on a bookshelf or what
is adrift on the floor
but something
has eased, you
are no longer
prisoned
in black

that
is how I think
hope will look
when hope creeps back.

A Woman Who Does Not Believe In Spells

gathers candles, hawthorn, sets a bowl
on the sill in a certain place so that water
can draw moonlight into its centre

she does not believe in this but is broken
by injections, hormones, scans, the pinpricks
of pity in the consultant's voice   feels herself

shrivelled from a person to a failed procedure
the tides of her body were lunar once, might
this huge-bellied moon hold a child in its gift?

she does not believe, but what is a spell except
a different way of asking?   the woman
opens the window wide   wider

TALKING ABOUT THE WEATHER

At 2 pm and 2 am our thread of words
stretches between hemispheres

I tell her it's mild, the wisteria buds
fatten every day, she tells me
she's got a stack of firewood in
has picked apples, mushrooms

dry though I say *the garden
already needs watering*
and she says *listen!*

half a world away rain hammers
against her iron roof, wind roars
I sit in my soft spring afternoon
and hear her winter sharpening its claws.

CAFF

I step into a density of frying
sausages, bacon fat, air so thick
you could cut slices of it, slap it
on a plate beside the eggs and beans.
The urn gusts steam, a coal fire stirs in
hints of smoke as through swing doors
breakfast after breakfast bursts towards
van drivers, bikers, high-vis jacket men who
jostle glances, keen to claim *black pudding, one without,
two large, one medium,* slabs of toast and mugs of tea.
I only
want
a coffee.
The woman at the counter
looks at me with an expression on her face
that says I've missed the whole point of the place.

ALSO ON CONNOR ROAD

When people say spring is beautiful
they don't mean round here
broken pavements chip-shop air
buildings sagging into
car-yard gardens
but I can hear
a blackbird
lifting notes
above the traffic
and look! next door
the old man who is ill
has come out of his house
he is holding his wife's hand
she is showing him snowdrops

ON NEW STREET I SEE A MERMAID

she sits on a concrete bench
in the thin sunlight
as waves of people
break about her
    she sings
    she combs her hair
long black hair
so long it ripples
over her shoulders
down her back
to the edge
of the stained sleeping bag
she has fishtailed around her legs
    she sings
    she combs her hair
when she leans forward
her hair is a black tide
spilling over her household
of plastic bags
    she combs her hair
    she sings
her voice dives
into the surf of traffic
swims through the hurry
of suits and mobile phones
    I cannot make out her words
    but I think
    she is singing
of how it feels to be beautiful
how it feels to be shipwrecked

Bird Feeders

Hung where I can watch
the flutter of robins,
sparrows, quick bright finches
as I wash dishes or make coffee

today the sparrowhawk
is also watching

he is carved stone on the shed roof
a gold stare locked to the feeders
sooner or later
the little birds will come

did you know I say to him
that 'musket' is the falconers' name for your kind?

the sparrowhawk ignores me
waits like a gun.

FORGETTING

It might be useful. I might
forget to be terrified of dogs
not bolt, sour-mouthed with fear,
when next door's Doberman lunges
at the gate. I'd call him good boy,
mean it, lean in to scratch his ear.

It might be magical, books
I know by heart growing mysterious
as unopened gifts. And if I can't recall
disliking thrillers or science fiction
will I tumble into marvels when
I forget what I prefer and read them all?

What if I forget my fear of flying,
catch the headiness of airports, wine
before breakfast, forgetting I disapprove?
What if, decanted into Barcelona, I chat
to everyone, savour paella, forgetting
I don't speak Spanish, don't like foreign food?

It might be extraordinary
a second chance.
Imagine leaping up joyously
every time the music started
having forgotten to care what people think
having forgotten I don't know how to dance.

EDGE

Her bare legs dangle from the bridge
as if she might stretch
to splash her toes in some cool river
but it's thirty feet down
and trucks not water

she cannot feel the rail
clawed in her hands nor the wind
pulling her cardigan into pale wings
can only feel how all the words
shriek and swoop and quarrel in her head
like rubbish tip gulls

how to keep her balance among them?
the hard words that pushed her here
soft words that try to coax her home.

THE 15:30 TO BIRMINGHAM

She calls it out
a man, a man with wings!
she's gathered to her mother's lap
she's hushed and shushed
don't point, don't be so silly
but there is
there is

stag men
staggering through
festooned in cans and foolishness
in orange wigs, in hats, in lewd balloons
the groom, or so his t-shirt says,
twirls in a tutu
wings

we bury frowns
in newspapers, gaze sharply
at the landscape sliding by, we try
to ignore the shambling carnival
they're loud *it's barely 4 pm*
somebody says *it won't*
end well

only the child
lost in amazement
at such loveliness reaches wide-eyed
to catch the magic, touch it
before it stumbles out of sight
and perhaps
she's right

we could reach too
smile, laugh, bellow good wishes
join with roaring voices for a while, sing
until the carriage rocks with joy, for after all
this giddy, grinning, almost-married boy
has friends
has plans
has wings.

Another Conversation About Where I Should Live

In my mother's street each garden has a lemon tree
lemons everywhere, so many lemons
baskets at the gates of houses, free, help yourself

every time she visits she is horrified again
that in England I must buy them
so much, so much, more than a dollar! – for just one lemon

I say it scarcely matters when I need so few
she frowns, reminds me I used to make
lemon curd, lemon tarts, fresh lemonade

she wants to catch me closer, reel me home
today she baits her hook
with lemons.

WAVES WERE FOR OTHER KIDS

from other streets. We swam
in a stir of mud, a gasp of water
from cold hills

swam amongst rumours of eels
and drownings, felt riverweed
slide against us in uneasy fingerings. We

swam anyway. Plunged, spluttered, flung
ourselves wild from ropes to drop
through pools dark as caves

or flopped in slow shallows, eddying
past willows where our mothers
sat collapsed in shade. We

sprawled to dry by old tyres
beached in reeds. A litter of bottles.
A hover of dragonflies. And I

drifted home each time silt-tangled
breathing river on my skin.
I smell it still. Etched in.

11 August 1999

I had forgotten the eclipse. Birds fell into silence
a creep of grey, the colour bled from every sun-lit thing
colder, suddenly. I shivered. I had taken warmth for granted.

We were at the coast under a wind-clear sky, had barely
scrambled our clothes back on, laughing, salt damp,
I had forgotten the eclipse. Birds fell into silence

and I held my breath, peered upwards, marvelled
as the moon unravelled day into a ghost-scape
a creep of grey, the colour bled from every sun-lit thing.

Later it seemed a metaphor for grief. You told me
I was not your future. The world drained of colour, grew
colder, suddenly. I shivered. I had taken warmth for granted.

IONA

A wind-bright morning
you drop from the ferry's noise
into the calling of gulls

you are not travelling
as a pilgrim, you have come
for white sand beaches, coves
where water dances every shade of blue
you want to glimpse a sea eagle
hear skylarks, wheatears, watch
otters tumble amongst kelp

but there across the fields
is the great mass of the Abbey
waiting quietly

you pause

the air hums with prayer

Christmas Card From My Aunt

arrives on the first of June
yet still a gift, she's ninety
words waver amongst holly
her name, two kisses, one line

too early, too late
every day is fragile
no letter this time but
she writes *all is well*.

What Is Kept

this! as if
one perfect stone exists on the long wash of coast

and you have found it

ochre-coloured, veined with quartz
or sandstone, a hole through its red centre

to be pocketed home
with two shells and a nugget of sea-glass

dropped in a dish with all the gathered others
flint and granite, marble, schist

a clutter of small rocks
drowsed in dust

yet if I pick one up
I can hear the ghost-shift of tides on shingle

I can see you, beached in sunlight, choosing it

SONG FOR MIDSUMMER

I am standing
up to my armpits in cow parsley
and the sky is a shout of blue
I know
there are packages waiting
five or six at least
all of them addressed to me
all of them full of trouble
but I am not
in a hurry to open them
I'm going to stand a while longer
amongst dog roses and sweet grasses
hum half a tune, watch the shift
of fair-weather clouds
what shape
will that small cloud take next, do you think?
a door?
a suitcase?

The Pottery Bowl Speaks

extraordinary
to drowse through millennia
believe myself no more
than stolid particles of clay
and then!
scooped up
wrenched into light

can aluminium silicate gasp?
such shock to be touched, cupped
to feel the softness and slip of turning
dizzying to discover my molecules
held such plasticity
and all
so quick   so quick   so quick

even now, burned back into stillness
I keep the astonishment of it
the knowledge of hands
imprinted in my earth
how I was held
how I was shaped to hold

The Temperature In The Crater Lake

is rising
monitoring teams report
increased gas density strong tremors
this is a good thing
to talk about   if Ruapehu erupts
it is not my fault not your fault
lava flows
are a safe topic

it is even possible for us
to mention the past
when the past
is mudslides and ash clouds
thunderstorms of rocks
this is
mountain history
not ours

so let us discuss
pyroclastic currents
seismic activity
for the landscape of you and me
is scorched
unrecognisable
I do not know
if we can live in it

talk carefully

And What If He Does?

she has thought only of how she will feel
as his phone rings on and on, endlessly unanswered

but now the whisper in her head asks other questions
what if - what might she say - what does she want

once they talked as easily as breathing, spoke
of everything, even as he said hello she'd know
if he was sad or tired or lit with happiness

but now? perhaps she'll barely recognise his voice
perhaps she'll hear in it
how he has shut the door of his life against her

no she thinks   too late for fragile reconnections

but there it is
his number

and it beckons

The Gentleman Of Fortune

Luck at the bar, cocktail in a frosted glass, his third gin sling
but he is Luck, no hangovers for him

he's looking sharp - Armani, handmade oxblood shoes -
scrolling his iPhone Pro Max, flicking quick messages

four barstools down I try to catch his eye while not seeming
too keen or too desperate   although of course I am, who isn't

I think it's worked when Luck looks back at me, but his
is a blank bored stare, one eyebrow raised as if he's saying *really?*

and what's the offer this time, have you touched scraps of wood?
crossed your fingers, stroked some amputated rabbit's foot?

is it coins in a plastic wishing well, a four-leaf weed?   I'm Luck.
I can be bought, up to a point, but you are hardly in my league

he shrugs back to his iPhone, scrolling, making careless choices
about who gets the lottery numbers or the all-clear diagnosis

who gets the publishing deal, the meal, a job, a passport,
who escapes the wreckage, who is on the last plane out.

Mrs Davies Is Well Enough To Leave The House

Last time I walked through flutters
of blossom, now I'm stepping over
fallen plums, a squash of purple
fizzing with wasps

wind slices my neck but sunlight
shimmies across parked cars
and the air is spiced
with someone frying chips

my eyes unwrap the street
bursts of dahlias, a new-shaved hedge
the door at 43 changed to blue
a kaleidoscope of ten front gardens

before I achieve the corner shop
buy a paper from a man whose shirt
is the colour of ripe plums
rain later he says

as if a little rain could ruin this!
lime trees sing from the park
buses, shiny as promises, dance past.

FOR PLANTING

I walk on a pebbling
of acorns, beech mast,
bristled sweet chestnuts

sycamore seeds
wide-winged as angels
catch at my hair

there are berries
hawthorn, holly, yew,
a gleam of conkers

the trees
in stirs of wind
toss down their gifts

such possibilities!
I scoop a handful up, hold
a hedgerow, copse, a wood.

You Know It Is Over

when for your fiftieth he gives you
a handful of DIY vouchers from the hardware shop

when he leaves for a conference in another country
with an open ticket *extra days for networking*

when the extra days stack into a month
he ends his texts *xx* but will not answer your calls

when it has been two months and you
have no more bright excuses to offer the neighbours

when it is Christmas

when he sends a list of things he wants forwarded
his brown leather jacket, favourite suits, his hiking boots

when you wake braced against the wash of pain, then notice
how serene the house has become, how easy it is to breathe

when you get your hair cut short, sleek as a young girl's
when you hum to yourself as the workman changes the locks

RONDEAU FOR THE MIRROR

The mirror lies in wait for me
increasingly untrustworthy
I sidle past, for lurking there
is some old person, scrambled hair
gone grey, although from memory

my hair is brown. I ought to see
a face dew-fresh and wrinkle-free
but if I risk a glance to where
the mirror lies in wait

it rudely insists I'm elderly
too battered for gin and gaiety.
On my way out tonight I swear
I'm turning it to the wall. How dare
it try to insist that woman's me!
The mirror lies.

THINGS SHE TAUGHT ME

look! hoar frost
each branch, each bramble, every spike of grass
dripping silver, frozen into lace

she insists we stop
scrambles from the warm hug of the car
to stand and marvel, breathing ice

today the landscape is restitched
in greens and golds, leaf-lush, fields
barrelled with gathered hay

blackberries clot the hedges *look!*
purple sloes already the stir of autumn
even as we drowse through summer

noticing

For A Moment

we pause, all of us

the woman checking messages
as she tugs her spaniel along
a man unloading wood
me, lost in lists and plans
even the headphone-muffled paperboy

all of us look up

arrow after arrow
wild geese
low   close   their calls
sharp as frost

they skim the barn, drop from sight
below the roofline

where are they going?
says the woman

nobody answers, but for a moment
all of us
are present

WOMAN IN THE DISTANCE

I see her out most days. Flare of red skirt
old-man's mudded coat, a stoop that twists
her silhouette into a story-book witch

silver hoops in her ears, a turmoil of hair
as if she slept in ditches. When she speaks
it's bell-clear, crisp as a headmistress

although she seldom does. Just once told me
when she walks she's walking through her past
the farm, her horses, parents, husband, sister

as she spoke made sure I understood
she'd rather be with them, not me. Waited to see
which track I took, so she could take the other.

And will I also come to this? Lose so much
I no longer want the company of the living
prefer my ghosts?   Perhaps.   I keep my distance.

This Storm

wants damage
punches the chimney so hard
it sets the stove-pipe shuddering
quick insistent squeaks
like birds
or tiny chittering witches
the wind
thumps windows
slams the letterbox
bang bang bangs the back door
the chimney witches
mutter furiously
stir explosions of sparks
the fire roars for wood
I fetch a fine sweet-burning hawthorn log
and offer it to the witches
I ask them
to please make sure the roof stays on.

THE DAY OF THE ELECTRICIAN

He has come
    his name is Nick, he has a shabby ginger beard
    but I would not care if his beard was scarlet, I would not care
    if he was called The Impaler and galloped in
    on a battle horse, so long as he galloped in
    with a multimeter, lineman pliers
    and IET certification

for electricians are as rare as nightingales
    and the wind is sharp and the ground is sodden and my knees
    ache with the knowledge that winter is eager
    to settle in my bones I dream
    of regular hot water
    a heated living room

I am not naïve
    I know in tender new relationships there's a time
    when electricians make promises and I believe them
    honeymoon days before the slide into acrimony
    unforeseen problems, unimpressive progress, unobtainability
    of parts and an invoice that makes me wonder
    if I should sell a kidney

but today I will not think of this
    today I will rejoice
    that an electrician has come to my door
    at the hour - at more or less the hour -
    when he said he would come

I am giddy with optimism.

On the Matter of Perspectives

A warehouse has invaded our horizon
sprawled ugliness along the line of hills

surely you hate it too? this vast grey wedge
in place of trees, lights that corrupt our dark

but you say it looks like an ocean liner, glitters
at night as if it pulsed with jazz bands, cocktail lives

you talk of how its steel walls gleam pearl at dawn,
gather the shape of clouds, blaze with sunset.

Rose-tinted nonsense. And yet I put my anger down
almost hear, some nights, the soft drift of a saxophone.

In February

the widower comes knocking
brings pink cyclamen in a ceramic pot
offers of lunch

no she says
ducks out of his hug, his invitations
no sorry sorry

and she is
she knows him for a kind sad man
who wants to settle his grief with hers

but she is not ready
to let go of her aloneness
every day it shifts shape

some days
it is a crush of rocks so heavy
she can barely leave her bed

or a gale
storming through every room of her
blowing doors open

sometimes
it is a handful of sharp fresh herbs
she once knew the names of
might remember how to use.

WE MAKE SOUP

I slice and stir, trusting the old pan
to transform weary vegetables
into savoury rich-steamed bubbling

at my elbow the ghost of my mother
stands frowning, points out my knife is blunt
tells me to taste again for salt

still glad of her company, for she
says nothing today about grief and loss
the brutal avalanche of news

as if to remind me sometimes
it's better not to think too much
more use to prepare a meal

thick-buttered fresh-cut crusts
soup in a yellow bowl.

When you are sad

it is easier to talk to trees
than people. Conversations with trees
are slow and considered, it can take weeks
for a tree to answer, but the wait
wraps you in shifting light
the smell of sap and green leaves.

Trees have a great deal to say
their branches creak secrets, roots
weave messages through the earth.
But they do not mind if you have no words.
They accept silence as easily
as if silence was a beetle
or a small pale fungus.

Nor do you have to worry
what a tree thinks of you.
Trees are not interested in judgments
they take the long view and you
are such a momentary presence
transient, no more than a wren's nest
less than a colony of wood ants.

Indeed, while trees are sorry for your sadness
they wonder why you are so troubled.
Some seasons can be cruel
hard almost beyond enduring
but surely you know, no season lasts.
Droughts break.
Warmth creeps back.

Field Notes

Goldeneye she says
steadying small binoculars
green head, white cheek
a drake.

Her husband
does not shift his 'scope
just grunts
ridiculous
wrong time of year
common Tufted Duck or such.

The Goldeneye
shrugs, swims through rippled shadows
towards his pleasing sleek-feathered wife.
He gives the couple in the hide six months
not every species mates for life.

OPEN

Yesterday was gunmetal, hail
punching the afternoon like rivets
yet dawn opens milk-wash soft
blossom-pearled, swan-feathered
with small white towpath drifts
the cob grooming, curving
his great neck this way and that
pale as paper the sky waits
for today to be written.

POETRY PREVIOUSLY PUBLISHED

The following poems were first published elsewhere:

'Waiting for Optimism' *What Next* (Dempsey & Windle, 2020)

'A woman who does not believe in spells' *Hysteria 10*, 2023
Ed. Linda Parkinson-Hardman

'Forgetting' second prize winner
Grey Hen Press competition (2019)

'Waves were for other kids' *Not Past But Through*
(Grey Hen Press, 2021)

'11 August 1999' *Another Word in Your Ear*
(The Percival Guildhouse, 2025)

'For Planting' *Renewable Energy* (Grey Hen Press, 2022)

'Gentleman of Fortune' *A Word in Your Ear*
(The Percival Guildhouse, 2024)

'Mrs Davies is Well Enough to Leave the House' *Orbis* #205 (2024)

'On the Matter of Perspectives' and 'When You Are Sad'
in.spire (Fragmented Voices, 2022)